W   e!

Stop Waiting, Start Writing.
A Step-By-Step Guide to Turn
What You Know Into a Book

Cathy Presland

COPYRIGHT PAGE

ISBN 978-1-910054-00-0

A Big Book Project
Published by: The Big Book Project (find us at www.thebigbookproject.com)
Design by: Caroline King
All images: Shutterstock

For writers everywhere.
Because you can transform lives with your words.

Contents

This is the book that will take your idea, take what you already know, and show you how to turn it into a book. If you have an inkling, a kernel of an idea, a burning desire, or that breath of a dream that just maybe there is a book in your future, this is for you. If you want to write your non-fiction business-building book – something with impact, this is for you.

You might have thought about becoming a published author but you don't know if it is possible. Let me tell you that it is. Follow the process in this book and you will get the clarity, structure and belief that you can do it.

Introduction

There is a spark that ignites when you realise you can write a book. That your message, solution, or story is worth sharing, and it's much easier than you thought. But right now, you might have some doubt or uncertainty, or so many ideas swirling around you don't know where to start. Can I do it? How much does it cost? Have I got the time?

I understand that because I work with people just like you and I can help you create content that has value, that can be marketed, and that will grow your credibility, your reach, and your understanding of what you know and do.

What you get in this book is a roadmap to take your unformed idea, work it through a series of questions and reflections, and transform it into your book. You'll get clarity on what to write, you'll create a flow and structure, and find the confidence to start writing and the self-assurance to stay with it. It's also a practical guide. We look at costs and launch plans and how to avoid writer's block.

And it's a journey of self-discovery. Of consolidating your knowledge and expertise and becoming more visible. I don't believe in waiting to be picked. In the digital world, costs are lower and timescales shorter and no-one has to spend years with a dusty typewriter and a pile of rejection letters.

If you've ever thought about writing a book, then I urge you to do it. Your world will change when you realise how much value there is in what you know and how many lives you can touch. Half a day working through the content in this book might just make the difference between writing a book 'someday', and creating something you can hold in your hands tomorrow.

Cathy Presland
thebigbookproject.com

P.S. All of us can let simple errors slip by and if you see any errors or omissions then I apologise. Please let me know and I will correct them for the next edition. My future readers and I will be very grateful!

How to Use this Book

Action Steps:
To do

Notes:
Space for making notes

Highlight:
Highlighting key ideas

Post Its:
Ideas and brainstorming

Bubbles:
Headlines and quotes

Extra worksheets:
Available at
thebigbookproject.com

There are three parts to this book –

The Big Picture – your longer-term vision around what else you do in your business, career, or life. **The Book** – where we create the flow and structure for you; what content you include (or leave out); when you will find *time* to write? And, finally, **The Book Launch**. How you get the message out about your book – and how you encourage people to buy and share it.

The process is simple, you have a narrative journey and process to follow, with questions, and **Action Steps**. It's a guidebook. Which means it is a dialogue between you and me. It's an exploration of your ideas. You can read it through to absorb the process but you'll get the most out of it if you participate in the conversation by answering the questions. Reflect on your ideas, structure them, and – ultimately – take action on them because what you will uncover through this process is incredibly powerful.

Do you have to complete *everything?* That's up to you! You'll get the most value by working through the first two sections step by step – and maybe come back to the third later, when you're closer to launch.

I hope you will use this book. I hope you write in it. Colour in it. Paste pictures and reminders in it. See what is possible and then go for it. Write and publish your own book.

Truly – it is a thing of joy.

The Big Picture

01: **Start With Why?**

Why Do We Write?

When we write, we create something of significance.

A book has an intrinsic value that is worth more than the cover price. Our emotions around books are wrapped up in how we live and how we learn. The memories of childhood and the respect we give to teachers. Your book is also a statement of achievement. That you completed. That you have something you can be proud of and that you will be respected for. Your book can inspire, entertain, or educate someone; can communicate your solution to a problem so that the reader can grow their business, save money, get fit, eat more healthily, dress more fashionably, write better, find romance, or simply enjoy a few hours reading your content. A book doesn't have to be long to communicate your idea or story. Whatever your ambition for your non-fiction book, creating and publishing it can help you grow your authority, reach a wider audience, leave a legacy, and maybe even change a life. It can certainly change yours.

And the place to start this process is with 'why'. Everything you will write comes from *why* you do what we do. As soon as you identify this, you are more motivated and more inspired to finish when that first flush of enthusiasm and excitement has passed.

So for me, I help people write books because I believe everyone has something of value to say. I love to see the leap in confidence and the opportunities and connections that are created with a book. I also love the process of shaping and forming intangible ideas into something concrete. *What* I do is to teach and mentor and – I hope – provide some inspiration to help you take that leap. And *how* do I do it? I have books, training courses, I run workshops, and I lead small groups – bringing together individuals who want to write and self-publish their books. And occasionally I do some individual consultancy.

Action Step: Start with Why

The very first action step I want you to take is to find that 'why'. The reason you do what you do and the reason you want to communicate it. What's the bigger reason you do what you do? What's your 'why'? Is it to change lives? Is it to tell your story? Is it so you can have more time to spend with your children? Is it because you love the intellectual challenge? Is it because you believe good design is functional and you want to rid the world of bad design?

_____

_____

_____

_____

_____

And, why now? You may have been thinking about this book for months – even years. Why is now the right time?

_____

_____

_____

_____

_____

It's OK if some of your answers are still hazy or if you have more than one reason – just asking will help you find clarity and you can come back to this section whenever you want to.

02: **The Best Book for You**

There are lots of books you *might* write. But I want you to get to completion, and it's easier to do that if you're writing the right book. You start the journey with a creative intention; to express your ideas, experience, or story. And then you realise that it takes time and resources to finish – which is a big investment to fit around a full-time business or job, to say nothing of a personal life.

In this section, we uncover the best book for you, right now. Not every book you could write will have the same impact. Not every book will be as transformational for you or for your business. And not every book will sell as well.

There will be different books in your future and there are different reasons to write. Sometimes we want more creative expression – more of 'us' in our books. Sometimes we have a specific business ambition and we give more weight to that. There's no right or wrong, but there are three elements which need to fit together and I want you to understand them all before you start. It's very easy to find yourself in that place of 'Too Many Ideas', and getting clear now helps you stay out of distraction and actually get to 'The End'.

Your Vision	**Your Reader**	**Who You Are and What You Know**
This is about what else you do and how you want to use the book to help position you, to help market your business, or to communicate what you want to say. Get clear on your vision and direction. Whether that's for your business or your career. Or for a deeply personal reason – to tell your story or to share your message.	The second part is getting clear on your reader – who are you writing for and what does he or she want to know, or want to be inspired to do or achieve? What problems do they have and what solution can you offer? The more specific you are the more your book will be picked up, bought, consumed, and passed along to friends	And finally – since this whole process is to turn what you know into a book – we look at what you know, what you do, your experience, your story and what motivates you at a very personal level. You have more content than you think and realising this will give you confidence that you can get your book out quickly and easily.

If you can imagine putting these three pieces into overlapping circles, then your book – the book we're going to work on throughout this action guide – lies at the centre. It needs to contribute to your business (or life) priorities, it needs to connect with a potential reader, and it needs to communicate what you know, are passionate or motivated to write about. There's no point just writing what you know and finding that no-one wants to read it and – in the same way – I don't want you to write something you think is marketable but hate every step of the process.

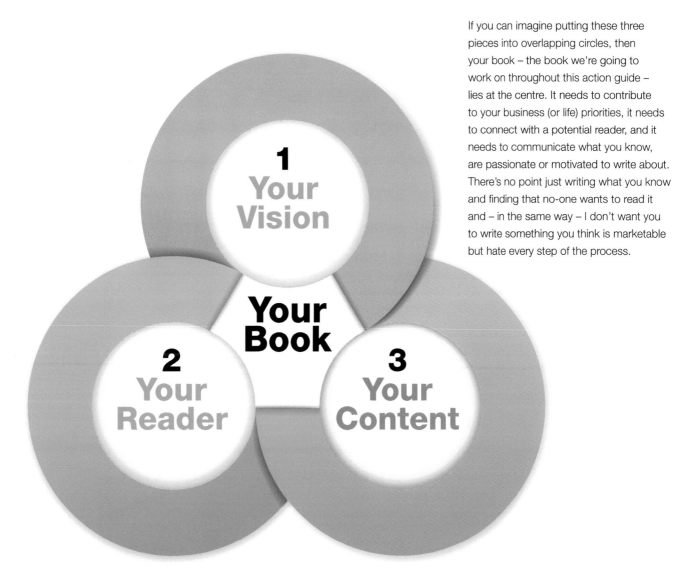

03: **Your Business Vision**

Now and In The Future

If you are clear on the direction you want for your business, your career, or your personal ambitions, then it's easier to be clear on the shape and content of the book that will take you there. There are many books you could write – and hopefully will write. But there needs to be a first or next book. First books especially can be the most challenging to write because you have so many (dare I say too many?) ideas. You may have a lot of experience by now, and it doesn't always fit into one book. Better to pick one book, complete it, and then move on to the next one.

Most People...

Most people who decide to write, start with the content. What they want to say. And you've probably already thought about your content. What are you going to write? Maybe you've started to make notes, or maybe you're part way through your book already. Then your reader's perspective comes in – sometimes. And often as an afterthought when we think about the marketing part. But if you flip this around – and do some strategic or big picture thinking *first,* or look a little further into the future, then you'll write a more powerful book. Creating and publishing a book takes time and energy – and money. Time especially is often one of the most precious commodities we have. Invest a little time now so that your book can repay you again and again for the long-term.

The Possibilities for Your Business-Building Book

It's good to look around at what other people are doing to get ideas for you business. While you're doing the action steps here, take inspiration from other businesses, or other innovations you see around you. I don't want you to copy ideas without considering whether they are right for you, but inspiration often comes when we see something new and it sparks our imagination. We might love it or hate it but we can adapt it. Ask yourself: *Who is offering something really innovative that might be a good model for me?* We're not talking about copying your competitors – sometimes the best ideas come from different industries or contexts – but innovation is often iterative, so be inspired by what else is going on around you. Let your imagination roll. And be savvy – if you see a good idea, ask yourself: *Can it work for me? Would I love to do it? How can I put my own twist on it?*

8

Keep a notebook with you so that you have somewhere to record your ideas. I think there's something powerful about the process of writing – and the time it takes to help us process our ideas – but in the age of technology you can also use a small voice recorder or an app on your smart phone.

Notes:

Action Step: See The Possibility

What have you seen other people doing and achieving with books that maybe you'd like to have for yourself? Ask yourself: How can I make them work for me? What is my perspective and what can I add to that idea? How can my book help me get there?

04: **Success: More Than Your Book**

Your book is just part of building your success. It's a vehicle to package your knowledge and expertise. I want you to think beyond the book towards what comes next. Here are some specific ways a book can be a business asset for you – let's see if any are a fit for you?

Get Noticed

Whether you have how-to expertise, or you're writing an opinion piece, a book is an easy way to share your perspective, demonstrate your credibility, and position you as the go-to authority or expert. Just by writing what you know, even if what you know is similar to other people in your industry, people will see you differently. And if you want to *really* stand out; to be the challenger or the new thought leader in your industry and shake things up, then a book is ideal. It can help you get noticed in a way that drives publicity and PR.

Maybe you'd like to use that positioning to start speaking, or raise your fees, of just get better introductions to higher quality clients, potential partners or new connections? The financial value of your book comes from what else the book allows you to do. Yes, you may get book sales, but more likely you want business connections to approach you because they know who you are. And this can lead to bigger consultancy projects, speaking invitations and other opportunities.

Those opportunities come alone without you even realising it was down to your book. I participated in a Women's Business Leadership seminar recently, and in conversation with the organiser about a book being a great business strategy, she paused. "I hadn't realised until you said it, but I think almost everyone I asked to speak has published a book." She hadn't consciously invited us because we were authors. But at some level, it made us stand out when she was selecting her short-list of speakers. And that's exactly the sort of opportunity that can come to you.

Notes:

Get Clients and Customers

A book can attract clients and customers to you rather than you finding them. With a digital book for sale on Amazon or one of the other online retailers, people who are looking for information on your topic can find you and get to know you by buying your book. If they enjoy your content they can click on a link and move over to your website. Maybe they could sign up for your email list, or buy another one of your products? This person is likely to be a great fit to become a client or customer because they have pre-qualified – he or she has taken the time to get to know a little about what you teach and wants to know more.

And this can work just as well in person. You're probably meeting potential clients and contacts all the time? Why not have copies of your book to give away, or sell, when you go to networking events or conferences? You don't want to thrust it on everyone you meet – just those who are interested – but how much more memorable is it to give someone a book rather than a business card? And a book isn't just about helping people find out about you. It also helps them know that you are the *right* person to work with. Your book is a physical reminder of you and what you do and hopefully they will at least flick a few sections to find out more about you and what you teach or do.

And for consultants or employees a book is like a mini-project proposal or a CV or résumé. It's something to leave with potential consultancy clients, or to send to a potential employer. You don't need to have the definitive book on a topic, just the fact you are a published author will help you stand out as the expert you are.

Get Sales

It isn't just about the book sales. I know we might dream about bestseller listings, but the reality for most of us (especially non-fiction authors) is that there is more potential in related revenue streams. You'll hear other authors talk about this – the money is in what else you sell – seminars and workshops, for example. Yes, of course, you want to write a book that gives you the best chance of long-term success – you want ongoing promotion, you want content that has longevity and will stand the test of time – you don't want to have to keep updating it, and bringing out new 'editions'.

And you can definitely help yourself here by promoting your book wherever you go, selling it at your workshops or seminars, or adding value to (and raising the price of) your training by including a 'free' book.

But for more serious financial return, think about *what else* you can offer that is related and complementary. We often read something, and then go on to read other books by the same author. Or we buy the person's 'system' – just think about food books or health books you might own.

You can do the same – use your book as a way to get the word out about your conferences, or your training courses. Or, if you don't have these yet, then can you create them? As you map out your book you might have ideas for more than one book – why not create a series, three or five books all on a similar topic so that you can build up your author empire step-by-step. This is perfect if you want to spend more time writing and less time out there networking.

If you look at the content in this book, you'll see that I can also run workshops around it. I can create a video course if I want to – similar to my other popular online training. I have choices in the *ways I deliver the material.* Don't feel you have to be constantly creating new material. Think about the different ways that more people can consume that same content. Audio books, in-person experiences, coaching and consultancy can all flow from the same piece of content.

Position for Transition

You may be at a place of transition. You may want to move out of your old career or job or business into something new. A book is a great vehicle to take you there. Write a book about your experience, your story, and use it to set the stage for something new and better in your life.

Action Step: Your Business

So with ideas flying let's start to get some of them down on paper.

Where is your business now and what products and services do you already offer for sale? If your book was going to be an invitation to just one or two of these, which would it be? Maybe you want to keep it simple and you just want more clients for exactly what you do now? Or maybe you'd like to expand and use your content in different ways? Develop training seminars or online courses?

Where, specifically, do you want to go next? If you stood here in three or five years' time, what do you want to be doing? What could that success look like? Do you want to stand out and get noticed? Maybe you want to be on a stage speaking or maybe you want to inspire a movement? How could your book expand the horizons for you? How could you engage your readers to help you get there? What do you want them to do when they pick up your book (buy it!), or as they read it (do you have something you want them to do or to go and sign up for?), and when they've finished (do you have some way they can get in touch?) It's likely to be about more than book sales for you.

If you want to make a transition, what is the transition you want to make. How could your book facilitate that for you – open up new opportunities?

Write your ideas down in this space.

05: **Your Reader**

It's Not About You
Really?

Yes, really. Some of us want to write the book about us, about our story. And sometimes that's a book that needs to be written. Once you understand why you want to write, then you can take a 360-degree look around you to identify who you are writing for and what his or her interests and concerns are. This is especially important if you want to sell books. Or you want to get clients. Your book is then a stepping-stone for someone to take action with you. It's like a conversation. The more it's about them, the more interesting it is. Yes, there are books that challenge us to think rather than to act, and you may be writing one of those. But most of us are writing something that is a solution to a problem. Or the gift of inspiration. Know what that might be before you write. And even if you want to write the rebellion book to wake-up your peers, the more you know about them the more engaging and contagious that book will be. What pushes their buttons and what do they believe to be true that you can challenge?

First Who

You will probably know who you are writing for although you may not have described him or her. It's likely to be the people you work or interact with every day. You could model this on a client, or someone you have trained, or even one of your facebook friends or other social media connections.

And what's your reader doing right now? What are they interested in right now? You can use a quick examination of what's selling on Amazon for example as a proxy for what people want to know or read. And therefore what they might want you to help them with. Getting clear on who you're writing for helps you get clear on what to write.

Action Step: Your Reader

Who are you writing to?

Not "Who is going to buy your book?" – you don't know that – and you probably want everyone to buy it. We're talking about the reader – the person you're talking to as you write. Although many different people will buy your book, you'll find it easier to write if you're writing for one person. If you can hold in front of you an image of that one person, your writing will also be more engaging. When someone does read your book it will be as if you are talking to them – because you are. You might not be able to answer all these questions, but have a go.

Use the space below to draw a picture of your reader, or to cut and paste some images from a magazine.

It may help for you to think about these questions:

Notes:

Who is she or he? Male, female, young or old? Who do they live with – a partner, children, anyone else home?

Do they work? Doing what? Do they love it or hate it?

How much do they earn? What are willing to spend money on (and that's different to what someone might say they are willing to buy!).

What do they do every day? Hobbies and interests. What are they reading? Listening to?

What goes on in their head? What do they believe? What are his or her values?

What kind of books or ideas turn them off? What presentation styles do they love or hate?

What are they feeling? What's the emotionally driven desire? What do they want to change in their life, business, health, relationships (not all of these are relevant but think about things beyond just your narrow topic. At some level, most people just want to be appreciated or loved.) Are they looking for a solution to a problem? A new perspective? To learn something? What is it?

Notes:

Then What

If you know what your reader is interested in and what his or her burning questions are, then your content practically writes itself. It becomes as if you are having a dialogue with your reader. We can all talk about what we do and what we know – we just need someone to ask the right questions – and the right questions are the ones your reader is asking. And the best way to find out what these are is to engage with them. Sometimes as experts, we think we know best. But the reality is that our reader is often at the beginning or much earlier in their journey than we are. He or she doesn't know what you know and if you make your content complex, they may not read it or engage with it as fully as if it is written at their level of understanding and experience. Put yourself in their position. Keep it simple is often the best mantra.

It can also help to understand what's selling – especially what books are selling well! Go onto Amazon or Barnes and Noble or into your bookstore and look at the popular books in your category. Which ones seem to be ranking well? Sometimes you can sort by 'popularity'. Ask questions. I was at a business conference last year where a large publishing house had a stand. I engaged the staff and asked them what was popular, which books were doing well that year. Use these opportunities like exhibitions and trade shows to find out what is working in your sector.

And what's topical? What's in fashion? In diet and exercise for example, it's all about interval training and mini-fasts. Do you want to ride on the back of this trend – maybe now is the perfect moment for your content? On the other hand, if you disagree with the current thinking, then say so. I had a client who was writing a book to guide people to a sugar-free diet. She was very critical of some of the popular authors in this space who advocate replacing sugar with low-calorie alternatives. That's her opinion and she is able to give clear reasons why she advocates that and it makes her position different, and therefore creates a talking point. This can make you and your book stand out. It can help you get good media coverage online and offline. Why is the new trend wrong? What does your approach teach instead? I'm not advocating being controversial for the sake of it but don't be afraid to stand firm in what you believe and know to be true – even if it positions you away from the mainstream. Be confident about your message and it can also help your marketing!

Content

Everything that is insid
In media production an
information and experi
provide value for an er
material, including tex
constitutes a publicati

How to Research Your Reader

You probably know your reader because you interact with him or her every day, or maybe he or she is an earlier version of you? But even if you think you know them, it's always best to check-in. Listen to people around you – on social media, in your business, in your networks. What frustrations do they have? What questions aren't being answered for them?

And try to go below the surface layer. Someone wants to lose weight. But why? Because they want to get fit. But why? Maybe they had a health scare and it frightened them. Maybe they feel less attractive as they get older. Ask more questions and listen more closely. If you can find this deeper reason, you will create a better connection with your content and write a better book.

Listen to Your Clients and Customers

You may think you know this but be open to asking. Offer your email list, or your connections, a 15 minute consultation on their most pressing question. Listen carefully (and of course offer advice if you can help them!). Take notes at your coaching sessions or consultancy meetings (with consent). Run a survey. Free survey software like Survey Monkey makes this very easy.

Get Social!

A lot of information is shared on social media. Join relevant groups or forums and ask for their ideas and concerns. There's a very simple function called facebook questions that lets people vote with a single click. And, without being a stalker(!), you can easily browse around people's interests on facebook, see what they are sharing on Pinterest.

Other People's Sites

Browse around popular websites in your field. What topics seem to be 'hot' right now. Where are readers engaging? Which blog posts are getting most views? Which are getting most comments? The most shares? Blog sites sometimes have buttons that tell you how many tweets or comments a post gets. And look at the comments on blog posts. What people say in response to a post is often better than asking them directly.

Action Step: What Are Your Reader's Burning Questions?

What is your reader looking for? Do they have a burning question, a problem, or a challenge?
Or are they just looking for some light reading or entertainment? Or maybe something to
challenge and stimulate their creativity or intellect? What's relevant or interesting to them?
What's topical? What's selling?

Identify your reader's most important questions. Then narrow the questions down to the
most important, or to those that you can best help them solve.

Highlight: Highlight the most relevant

06: **Your Content**

At this point, you know where you're heading, and you know who you're writing for and what interests them. It's now time to look inside yourself and look at what you know and what content you have – to identify your key teaching points, or your key messages. This is the content of your book.

What Do You Stand For?

This part of the process is about checking in with *you*. Yes you will write about what you know, but I also want you to write from a place of your values. Our best work comes from what we are really expert in, grounded in what we believe, and what makes us feel good. If we start here, then we will be more motivated, happier and more successful. It becomes easier to say yes or no to opportunities and to eliminate distractions. Your book will have one clear message and you will be able to stay true to that message as you write.

Action Step: Your Values

What are the most important values to you in your life?

Ask yourself what values help you do your best work, what values give you that greatest sense of happiness, of pride in what you do. Write them down.

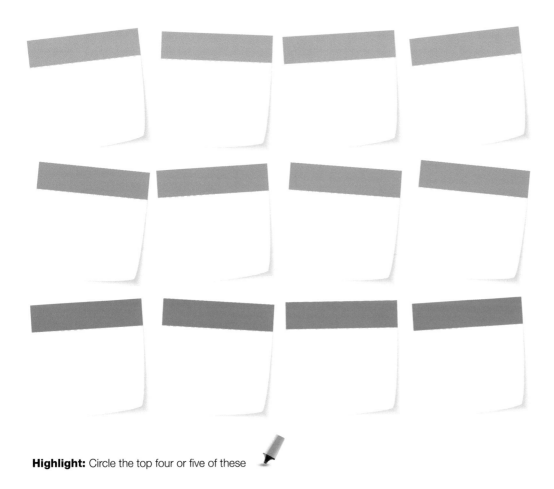

Highlight: Circle the top four or five of these

Action Step: Your Key Messages

We all have things that are core to what we teach, or points that we want to get over in the story we tell. What are these for you? Your core messages? Key principles guide your work?

So for example, you may be a nutritionist who believes that you must eat healthy natural food to perform at your peak, and you will never advise the use of supplements. Or you may be a business mentor who believes your clients should be earning a certain level of income before they invest in your services.

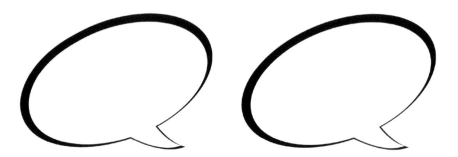

Why do people approach you and what is it they love about what you offer or what you talk about?

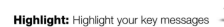

Highlight: Highlight your key messages

Notes:

Action Step: Boundaries

It's easy enough to talk about balance, but it's a lot harder to achieve. What else is in your life that's important to you? That you don't want to give up? Or that you want to create? What is important to you and what do you need in your life to make you happiest?

There may be things in your life that are not negotiable and it's important to know what they are. These are personal rather than your teaching principles. For example, you may not want to build a big business empire. Or, it may be important that you never travel without your family. You may prefer to work with a particular type of client because you get them the best results and they give you the greatest sense of satisfaction.

Or maybe it's important to you to set up a business with no clients, that allows you to write all day! List them here.

Create more of...	Move away from...
A fully international business	Long term clients

Your Content – Turn What You Know Into A Book

And we all have a lot more content than we realise. You have content, even if you don't realise it, or even if it's in your head. Most of us aren't writing a long academic piece that requires years of research – we're writing from what we know, from our experience, from our story, from the stories of people we've worked with. We're creating frameworks, content, and advice gained from our expertise. We might need to check a few facts, or gather some background or stories, but we can write a good first draft of our book from what we know or what we have. So how do you turn what you know into that book?

Action Step: Identify What You Have

Start making lists.

What content do you HAVE?

Training courses, teleseminars or webinars, that free pdf ebook, worksheet or materials you use with clients... Maybe you can simply package what you have into a book – use content from your blog for example?

_____

_____

_____

_____

_____

_____

_____

_____

What do you KNOW?

What is in your head? Your coaching process. Your personal journey. Changes you want to inspire in other people. One hundred and one book ideas!

_____

_____

_____

_____

_____

_____

_____

_____

_____

_____

What do you not yet have or know but can access pretty easily?

Interviews with experts, client case studies, research materials.

_____

_____

_____

_____

_____

_____

What have you done recently that was captivating and fun? That you found personally and professionally fulfilling?

Think about which of your conversations, or events, or blog posts really engaged people around you. It isn't always the things that we think will get the most attention that do. Start to notice what people say about what they most loved. This is what will make your book stand out. That will bring your personality into play and reach the right reader for you.

Use the space below to write your core messages and what content you have or know that could be the starting point for your book.

07: **Bringing Your Book Together**

Prioritise

We now need to bring all this together and identify your one book. The book that's most important right now, that will move you forward in your business, and that engages with the problems or desires of your reader. Use this action step to narrow down your ideas to one book; one book that has one clear message.

Action Step: One Book

1. *How can the book help you position yourself and grow your business? Look at the list from page 15 and then prioritise. Identify just one. What is it? Maybe it's more clients. Or higher fees. Maybe it's the big stage. Maybe it's to help you move towards online courses. Or setting up long-term income streams so you can have more financial security as you move towards retirement. Write it in the one of the circles opposite.*

2. *Look at the ten questions you answered on page 23. If you had to answer just one, which is the one that frustrates them most and that you feel most qualified to answer? This is the question that becomes the Big Promise of your book – the outcome or result that you will deliver on. Write it in another of the circles opposite.*

3. *What about you? What content do you have that is a perfect match for this book? What is the easiest content to access, or the content that excites you the most? Write it in the last blank circle opposite.*

Getting clear on this part means it is much easier to shape your content and the way you write to get your book done. In the circles above, note your one (or possibly two) priorities for each of those pieces we looked at. And so what is that book that you are going to write? Is it clearer to you than before you started this process?

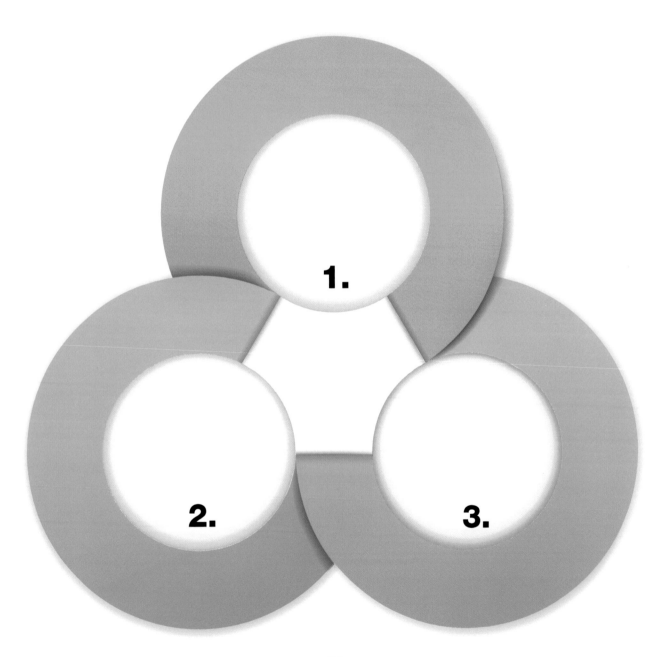

Notes:

Optional: What If I Can't Decide?

We all have more than one book that we can write. At some point, you'll find you could write two books. Or ten books. But the rest of this book is about planning your perfect book for *right now*. You just have to decide what that is. Which one is speaking to you now? Which one do you feel most inspired to write? Maybe it's the one that feels easiest for you (because you have the content perhaps?) Or the one that will be a stepping-stone to a new part of your career or life? Or the one that will get you the most attention and raise your visibility for speaking engagements?

You can be strategic – which is likely to position you or your business best? Where do you want to be in a year's time? And what might come after that – some people will have a whole series of three, four, or five books planned out. Or you may very emotionally drawn to one particular book. One that *has* to be written. Ultimately you have to go with what feels right for you. Which one is that? Which is the story you want to tell? What excites you most? Inspires you? Which message needs to get out now?

And it sometimes happens that you get part way through and then another book comes along that just *has* to be written and you decide to change. That's the way of books some-times. However, try to focus on completing one and then your second will fly from your fingers much more easily. If you haven't already identified your book then answer these questions to narrow it down.

Which makes the most 'sense' for your business?

Which 'feels' right? Which resonates with you the most?

If you looked forward three years from now, which book would you regret not writing?

You might get different answers to these three questions and will have to base your decision on what's right for you at this point in your business or career. Do you want to write the business-building book that will get you on national television? Or do you really feel there are things that need to be said and you don't want to regret not sharing them. Forget about the should. Think about it like a timeline. Which book will you write now and which book might come next? And the great thing is that you get to decide! You're the expert. You know your stuff. And at the end of the day, you have to write it. Go with your gut. Trust in your internal guidance system; the reality is that we just get a sense of what feels right. Really, the worst decision you can make is to stay in indecision. It's better to start.

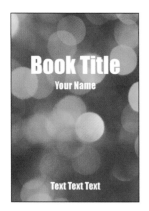

08: **Your Book Title**

Action Step: What's Your Book Called?

What's the title of your book? First thought, best thought!

You probably know the title of your book even if you don't realise you do. Get your first idea down. A working title. That's good enough. That's where you start. Write it down here and draw out your cover picture if you want to.

(If it helps you to sketch an image or cut something out of a magazine to help you visualise the book then please go ahead. This is your space to do what you like with!)

Capture That Feeling

How does that it feel with your name and your title on a book cover? Does it make it more real to you? Can you see how it will take shape? Really believe that it can happen? Hold on to those feelings. Use the cover you just sketched as a reminder that your book will soon be finished. Take a picture of the previous page with your iPhone and make it your background or screen saver. Or print out that page and put it on your desk or on the wall in front of wherever you plan to write. Or mock-up a dust jacket you can put over another book.

You may even want to commission a designer to create a cover for you? It may or may not become your final book cover – but it definitely helps make it real to have that constant reminder and inspiration as you write. How does feel now? To hold it in your hands?

Pretty good I hope!

Congratulations: You have taken the first steps in moving from your unformed idea to actually creating and writing your book. These are big steps and you should pause and capture the moment.

Notes:

09: **Funding Your Book**

How Much Will It Cost To Write My Book?

We may not think about the money when we're in the creative flow. But there are very real costs involved in finishing and self-publishing your book and it's a good idea to know what these are and work out how you are going to fund them.

Writing a book starts out as a creative pursuit. A passion. A desire to write, to communicate. It's about the writing. But at some point, it becomes a business venture. And like a lot of things we do in business it's a question of time or money – or both. Even as you are writing, that's time that you could be spending on other tasks or with clients. Or at work if you have a job. Or if you are writing around that, in the evenings or early mornings, then you're taking time that you could be spending with family and friends, or by yourself at the gym for example.

Hold on to the thought that it's an investment in your future. And it's also a very fulfilling project – you are creating a book! So many people want to do that and so few do. The process of writing, of putting your content out there, will help you grow in confidence, it will deepen your understanding of your content, and it will drive your business forward.

At some point you'll need to do the sums and find the money to self-publish. Allocate some costs and find creative ways to cover them – and some of the ideas might help you create a better book in the process. There's a lot you can do yourself for zero cost – just a little investment of time and maybe some learning. But there are a couple of places I always recommend some investment – as you'll see. Plan and cost it like any other project and consider how you can generate funds for your book before you create it.

Writing and Editing

Writing equates to time and your time is valuable *because of what else you might be doing.* Invest time in your planning and get the right support and you will finish faster.

And then there is editing. A structural editor will give you feedback about the overall flow of your book while a copy-editor or proof-reader will go through your work line-by-line and word-by-word for grammatical sense and spelling errors.

I *always* recommend you use a good editor – or at the very least a proof-reader. It's a rare person who sees his or her own errors!

- Coach or structural editor $1-$3,000+
- Talk and transcribe $200-$500
- Copy editors or proof-reader $200-$500+

Design

A book is judged by its cover so please invest in a good cover design. If you don't know a designer then try **99designs.com**

Format your work properly for whatever publishing medium you choose. Length and complexity of your interior layout, images or diagrams will all make a difference to the cost here.

Simple is best for digital publishing such as Kindle. Formatting for print will cost more but you can be more creative with diagrams, images, graphics, and tables to get a better look and easier usability.

- Cover design $200-$500+
- Formatting for kindle $100-$300
- Formatting for print $100-$1,000+

Self-Publishing Costs

If you self-publish and upload your own documents then the cost is practically zero.

Digital publishing has a very small learning curve and you will take home more of the royalty. Check out my site at **thebigbookproject.com** for resources.

For print copies, use Print-on-Demand (POD) services like CreateSpace, or Lightning Source. Your book is printed when someone buys it so no need for boxes of books in your garage! There are set-up fees but these are small.

Or you can find companies who will take all of this off your hands but that can come at a cost.

- Kindle and digital, practically zero
- Print on Demand $100-$200
- Get a quote before you commit
- Self-publishing company $200-$3,000+

Notes:

Book Launch

It can be a good idea (and a lot of fun!) when you launch to have some kind of in-person event.

You'll need to budget for event costs and also for print costs if you want to have your book with you (I'd advise this).

For single copies, POD services are likely to be more affordable. For a few hundred copies, get a quote from a local printer.

If you have an event, there will be costs, but why not make it cost neutral by looking for sponsorship, or asking a small entry fee?

Or do some hard negotiation with your venue. Maybe they'll let you have a room for free on a quiet Tuesday? Or there's always a local coffee shop!

- Launch event – $2-$5 per book
- Event – sponsors or small charge
- For tight budgets think online

Marketing Costs

If you're savvy online then you can do a lot for little more than the cost of your time.

How about a virtual party, some giveaways, special offers or bonuses? Or a free or low-cost promotion? All of this is very easy to organise.

Offer your book for sale to your networks or email list for the cost of print and P&P (people do love to hold a hard copy in their hands). And price this so that it comes to less than the cover price (because people do love a bargain!)

The more elaborate your marketing plans the more you should budget. But with creativity, imagination, and a little investment of time, you can do a lot for very little.

- Online events don't cost anything
- Offline PR is great but costly
- Be creative – video, blog tours…

Action Step: What Does This Add Up To?

There's always a bit of a reality check involved when we think about our book budget. But hopefully you are pleasantly surprised rather than scared off? Whatever your comfort zone you should be able to find a way to do this. If you're starting out and you don't have a lot to invest, then it's perfectly possible to do this for just a couple of hundred dollars or pounds. It's better not to do it yourself of course – and in that case your professional team will need a budget of a few thousand dollars (or pounds).

1 Writing and Editing

Design and Formatting **2**

3 Self-Publishing

Launch and Marketing **4**

Total

What Are My Funding Options?

And then there's really no need to find all the money yourself. If you hadn't realised – or hadn't budgeted – for the costs involved, then let's just look at some creative ways to fund your book. Try to find ways to raise money in advance. At least to cover some of the actual expenses, even if not the whole of your time. If you have some resources secured in advance, then you'll be more relaxed and secure about taking the time to write. Here are a couple of options for you...

Make The Money

Save a proportion of fees from your clients or a percentage of your income and set it aside until you reach your target. Have a sale on your products or services or hold a special event where all profits go to your book.

Or pre-fund your book. Offer an advance copy for sale before it's written and encourage take-up with bonuses (video training, or some live or online workshops?). This is a great way to test whether people are interested in buying and will also create buzz.

Get creative – there are so many extra products and services you could offer. Give someone a reason why and they are more likely to buy.

Crowd-Funding

This is where you ask people to buy a stake in what you are selling before it is created. It's different to pre-selling because you typically don't know the person and it's done through a dedicated crowd-funding site or service like Kickstarter or Pubslush.

Your 'investor' pledges money in exchange for the promise of a return or an advance copy of your product. The value you offer should go way beyond the cost of just pre-ordering your book. These sites usually allow different levels of rewards – 20 books for $100 versus you fly out to deliver a service in person for $20,000.

Have some fun – the more creative your campaign, the more inspired people will be to invest and the more likely it is to go viral.

"There are always more ways to fund your book..."

Notes:

Co-Creation

How about co-creating a book with someone who has different resources to you? I've done this with online training. I understand the technology and how to get the product to market. And working with an expert who has related content works well for both of us.

Or maybe you can facilitate a group and share costs? Create an anthology? It's shared content, your co-authors have a stake in the book, which makes it easier, plus they can help you market it.

Share the work, share the cost, share the credit. Just be careful when it comes to sharing royalties – it can be very complex to administer and better you keep it simple.

Sponsorship

What about asking for funding in return for publicity? If you have great content and a way to reach people someone else wants to reach then this could be for you.

Look at large companies in your field, professional associations, or individual high-profile celebrities.

Go back to what else your reader is buying – not necessarily in your industry – think wide.

Define what you are offering – is it a logo on the cover, a credit, a whole chapter? How long do you want the relationship to last? One print run? Forever? A certain number of copies sold?

If you ask there is at least a chance of someone saying yes!

Notes:

Can I Really Ask For Money Before The Book's Written?

This is a common question. And of course, you must act in alignment with your principles. However, so long as you have checked all the regulatory considerations, and have the right terms in place for refunds if for some unexpected reason the project does not go ahead then, yes, you can be paid in advance.

What is unknown is often intimidating and once you know what costs you might be facing, it's much easier to find solutions. And beyond that – it's actually a great way to check that people really want to read what you want to write about. It's easy enough in the isolation of your computer to think that you know. But you really don't know until someone hands over hard cash. Plus there is no better motivation to finish quickly than having paying customers waiting for your book to be ready!

Action Step: Fund Your Book

Using the ideas we just worked through, write down three ways you might be able to fund your book. Under each, write one actions you can take to move it forward.

1. *Funding Option: - Action I can take?*

_____

_____

_____

_____

2. *Funding Option: - Action I can take?*

_____

_____

_____

_____

3. *Funding Option: - Action I can take?*

_____

_____

_____

_____

10: **A Mini Celebration!**

One thing I think we don't do enough of – in general – but particularly in business and especially with writing – is to celebrate.

We're often too ready to jump in with self-criticism. Or too quick to move on to the next project. So let's just stop for a moment and take stock of what you've done and how far you've come. You've identified your book. You have your ideas in some sort of shape. You know who you are writing for and what he or she wants to read. You know what's selling. You know what's topical. You know what knowledge, content, and ideas you have. Wow – you have all of the pieces you need to start your book. And rewarding yourself is part of what will keep you motivated through the next stage.

We're not finished yet but you've reached a big milestone and I give you complete, unqualified permission to be proud of the work you've done. And to celebrate. To go out for a meal. To take a day off. To go out with a friend. To just sit and look at what you've done already and let the reality of your book really sink in.

Action Step: What's Your Celebration Going To Be?

If you write it down it's more likely to happen. What's your celebration going to be?

At the end of this chapter:

- You know why you are writing and why now is the right time for your book.

- You can see beyond the book to what else the book will bring you – connections, a career or business change, a bigger platform, or just a way to tell your story.

- You're really clear about which is the best book for you – the best fit for your business (or to help you get your message out), the best fit for a potential reader, and most closely aligned with you, what you value and what you know and do.

- You have a working title for your book and the process seems real and – hopefully – achievable.

- You also know how much it might cost to self-publish and – importantly – how you are going to fund those costs!

The Book

11: **Getting Started**

So now, the book stage, the one you've been waiting for. We're moving from the big picture of your life or business to the flow and structure for your book. You know *what* you're going to write, *who* you're writing for, and how it all fits with your bigger business or life vision.

Let's now go deep into your content and plan *exactly* what you are going to write about. Let's map your content, your chapter flow, your headings and sub-headings and actually create a detailed book outline. This means all that's left for you after that is to fill in a few gaps. It isn't quite writing-by-numbers but it's pretty close!

Bringing Shape and Flow to Your Ideas

Your reader needs a map. Imagine that your book is taking your reader on a journey. It can be your story – the classic hero or heroine story – your experience of struggle and triumph. Or it can be your reader's journey – a solution-focused book that delivers the outcome and results they want, and talks about the issues and challenges they will experience. Whichever it is, putting together a flow for your book is critical. This is the heart of your book plan. If you imagine it like taking someone on a guided walk. Your reader may know the destination but they don't know *how* they're going to get there. And they don't know what sights and experiences you have planned for them along the way.

In this book for example, I promise to give you an outline and a plan for your book. I promise that by mapping out your book it will be easier to write. I promise that you'll get clear on what to write. You'll get the book that is the best fit for your business, and you'll be ready to go away and start writing.

Action Step: The Destination

First, define your destination. Where are you taking your reader? What's the Big Promise or the big message of your book? This is the answer to your reader's single most important question. If you had one – just one – thing to tell your reader, to teach them or to solve for them, or one main story to relate, what would it be?

If you have more than one thing then write them all down but pick one. (Remember – you can write more books...). Circle the most important place you want to take your reader or the single most important result you are promising to deliver in your book.

Highlight: Circle the most important

12: **Walking Your Outline**

Now you're clear about the destination, you will walk – literally – the path that you're taking your reader on to get there. It's just like getting in the car for a routine trip, you know exactly how to get to your destination – it's an unconscious knowledge – and what we're doing here is getting that unconscious knowledge about your book down on paper – a bit like creating a sketch map. It's where all the work you have done up to now comes together. And there are three parts to it – first we *map* the overall, high-level flow of your book, then we *collect* all the ideas that will (or might) become your content, and then we *structure* them to create a detailed outline.

If you haven't done this kind of activity before it can seem a little unusual. No flip charts involved; no forms or worksheets to complete. But it works because our amazing brains have been processing all the work you've done so far. All you are doing is putting that information into an order, as if you were having a conversation – explaining to someone how to do something or relating what happened in the past

Think about those occasions when you forget something – a name or a fact. Then hours later, without you realising where it came from, the name pops up or the fact comes back to you. This is exactly the same. Even though you haven't been conscious of it, you've been processing ideas, reflecting on the work you have already done. We're just getting those ideas out in a sequence and creating the bare bones of your book.

Equipment: Don't Do This Alone
You can't do this one alone. Ideally, you'll have a partner, someone who can ask the questions and take notes as you talk. But in case you don't have someone else to hand, you can do it with a voice recorder or a voice-recording app on your phone. Whichever you choose, don't interrupt the process by taking your own notes. Do this with your eyes closed and stay in the flow.

Action Step: Step into Your Book...

First, stand up. You'll need room to walk forward a few steps.

And I'm going to ask you to talk aloud so you'll need some way to record yourself or have someone there to write down what you say. If you're on your own, use a voice recorder. If you're working with a partner, make sure they have pen and paper. Index cards or post cards are great for this. Ask them to write your 'verbal headlines' onto one side and the words or questions or answers that follow onto the other.

Make sure you have uncluttered space in front of you. Close your eyes. Imagine you are talking to your reader. Really picture the person you are writing to as if they were standing in the room with you asking questions. They ask you that single big question. How to get to that destination you've promised.

What's the first thing you want to say? The first part of your process or any background your reader needs to understand? It can work really well to have your buddy ask you this out loud "What's the first thing you say to them?"

As you ask the question of yourself, **take a step forward** *and as you move, say the answer aloud. Don't try to think about it – the words will come. Just let them. And have you partner write them down, or record yourself.*

Keep your eyes closed, and ask (or let your buddy ask), "What comes next?" Again, as soon as they've asked you the question, take another step, and as you take it, say what comes into your head. Don't pause and wait for the answer to come to you before you take a step. Just go with the process.

And carry on, until all your ideas are down on paper or captured on tape.

1. First
2. And Then?
3. What Comes Next?

13: **Your Table of Contents**

What you have now is the flow of your book – effectively your list of chapters. The actual chapter names may change as you write, but the structure of your book is now in place. What I want you to do now is write out your **main chapter headings** – a formal place to capture the 'walking' exercise you've just completed.

_____

_____

_____

_____

_____

_____

_____

_____

_____

_____

_____

_____

_____

14: **Collect Your Ideas**

Notes:

Now we have your chapter outline, we need structure *inside* each chapter, because a clear structure makes the writing easy. Without this, your book might never get finished. With it, you can have a first draft written in a couple of weeks. And a final draft off to your editor within a couple of months at most.

It's about breaking it into manageable chunks. If I asked you to write a book – a whole book – you might retreat into overwhelm. But if I asked you to sit down and write a couple of paragraphs, something about the length of a good quality facebook post or a blog post, that probably feels a bit different? I know that when I'm clear in my head, it's very achievable to rattle off 1,000 words in about twenty minutes. And writing a book is simply putting those short segments together with a flow and depth that tells a bigger story. And finding this flow, putting it into a structure will give you a sense of ease when you sit down to write.

Big Picture or Detail?
Imagine there is a line, and you have to put yourself on that line somewhere between being a big picture person and a detail person. Most of us will cluster at one end or the other; we have a preference. And this will affect how likely we are to think about and organise our content. Do you like to see things laid out step by step in a logical order? Or are you someone who loves concepts and moves quickly from idea to idea? For whom detailed instructions seem a little restrictive?

Because we're all different, I'm giving you two ways to collect your content together. Choose one of these methods or – if you're still not sure – then try both and see which you like best. Or use a method you already know and love. Either way is fine – but don't skip this part. Even if you've already started writing, if you create a structure, you're more likely to complete quickly and less likely to get overwhelmed with new ideas and a seemingly ever-growing project. If you have part-written content, just slot it into the right section. Perfect. A little bit of time invested at this stage will save you a lot of time if (or should I say when!) you have a day when you wake up and don't feel like writing. Structure overcomes writer's block better than anything I know. Trust me.

15: **Get Your Ideas On Paper**

Choose one of these methods to brainstorm all your ideas. We're then going to select the best and slot them into your chapter outline. Remember both ways are fine, it's your preference which to use. This is a day to get out the post-its, the paper and the coloured pencils. Yes, you can do this on the computer but it's very powerful to actually write on paper or on a whiteboard. It's like cooking or painting – be prepared to get a little messy in order to have the most fun!

If you need some prompts then think about: your reader's problems or frustration, his or her questions. What are the things that he or she needs to look out for? What other questions might they have?

Action Step: Plan Your Content

*Use **one** of these methods to plan your content, or use your own favourite planning method.*

Create a Mind Map
If you are a detail person, you'll probably love mind maps. A mind map starts at the centre and expands out, like a tree -- with branches and more branches off that. The concept helps you dig deep into a topic and go from broad to narrow. You'll want to start with your book title at the centre of the mind map, and then create a branch for each topic.

Then for each sub-topic. Go down to two or three layers of sub-headings if you want to. You can do this on paper or on a computer-based programme like Mindjet, iMindMap, or Mindmeister, or just on a large piece of paper.

Post-Its

If you are a big picture person then you might prefer one of my favourite methods for getting anything mapped out – the post-it. I love this because it lets me move rapidly between ideas and concepts, and to go wide rather than deep. There is merit to both methods, and both take you wide and deep, just that the way of thinking is different. You can also do this by writing on a whiteboard or chalkboard, or on a large sheet of paper, but I love post-its because I can move them around, group them and re-organise them.

Get yourself a pack of post-its and write one idea or questions per post-it. Write fast, don't think. When you start to run out of ideas, take your post-its and group them into topics that seem to make sense together on a large piece of flipchart paper, a whiteboard, or on a wall. They'll naturally fall into topic areas that make sense to you.

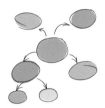

Use these pages to collect your ideas or draw your mind map.

THE BOOK

16: **Create Your Outline**

Having a clear structure for your book makes it easier to write and is more accessible for the reader. Many of us love long narrative fiction or non-fiction, immersing ourselves in the flow of a great book. But if you want to read a short thought piece, or a how-to book, ask yourself: what kind of structure and content draws you in?

Most people say they like books with headings, short sections and chapters that are easy to read, that invite you to continue section by section, to dip in and out, and learn what you need or enjoy a story or two. Some readers will skim – maybe before they buy – or maybe to get the meat of the book before diving in to read it all.

Structure your book for easy navigation so your reader can get to the essence and devour and delight in your material. Well-structured is more likely to be well-read. And when you start to write, short sections make it easier to complete. It's very motivating to tick off section after section, and it can feel as if your book is practically writing itself. Do the work now and save time and stress later.

Action Step: Map Your Content to Your Outline

Now that you have all your content ideas and your chapter outline, all you need to do is to map one across to the other. It's about this point you'll be starting to transfer your outline into a document. You might prefer to start in a word document, in Scrivener (which is a word-processing software designed for authors), or on paper. However you do this is fine. Take the information from your mind map, or the exercise that you did with post-its, and just slot it into the chapter and section where it's a right fit.

It can be a good reference point for you to do it here so that all your book ideas are in one place and you can come back any time you want. It's a reminder of the journey you are going on. Take your table of contents and leave some space under each. Insert your sections and your sub-headings so that your book starts to take shape.

Use the space below to create your **full structure and table of contents,** using the chapter titles you 'walked' out and add headings and sub-headings from the 'content' exercise.

17: **Make It Even Better**

And once you have a first outline, you can make it even better. Go through each of these principles, and edit and amend your outline.

Good Books Have a Clear Message

It's very tempting to want to include everything. Especially if this is your first book. Try to resist. Your book does not need to be long – 30,000-50,000 words is fine for a short non-fiction book and 15,000-20,000 words is great if you're planning a digital book.

Action Step: Be Ruthless

Now we have all your ideas on paper, it's time to be ruthless -- to organise and select the ones that will make it into your book. Your content should support the main point of the chapter. And your chapter flow should deliver on the Big Promise, the journey you are taking your reader on. Reflect on your headings-and sub-headings, and ask if they are an essential step in your process or story. If not, delete them, or put aside for the next book.

Questions Make Writing Easier

As you made notes and collected your ideas, you probably used words and phrases, statements of fact. Well, now I want you to re-frame those headings and sub-headings into questions, so that whenever you sit down to write all you need to do is pick a question and answer it. Imagine you are talking to your reader, that you're answering a question he or she has. Think of it like a conversation, and you can – literally – talk to them if you want to. Get a voice recorder or a software like Dragon Dictate. Talk or write out what you know or what you think. So if you're writing a book on *How To Run Your First Marathon Over Fifty*, then don't just have a chapter called *Shoes*. Instead, use headings like *Which Are The Best Shoes For A Beginner?, How Much Do I Need To Spend On A Pair Of Shoes?, How Long Will My Shoes Last In Training?*, etc. All of these questions will fall out of the action step you did, this is just about flipping it into a question format. Can you see how it will make the writing easier? Even if you change the headings later, do it this way now so you finish your first draft quickly.

Action Step: Use Questions So You Know What to Write

Notes:

I hope this is self-explanatory but go ahead and do it! Make all your headings and sub-headings questions that you can answer when you sit down to write...

Use Stories to Engage Your Reader

A good non-fiction book is not just a statement of facts and data. And it's not just a work of fiction or story-telling. It's actually both. Your non-fiction book will be more powerful if you can weave in stories. They can be your stories, or they can be other people's stories. And there is no single rule or way to do this. The balance of fact and story will depend on your reader. Is he or she driven by logic and facts? Or will they engage with the story telling and the emotional journey you relate?

A good story well told. This is true even in non-fiction. Weave your story or structure throughout the book. If you have something coming then plant a teaser for it – maybe at the end of the chapter or section – something that makes your reader want to read on.

Facts or opinions organised around a good structure. A good structure that helps you reveal the facts or the teaching in short sections that move the reader through your content in a way that gets the best results for them.

I often use the analogy of those big blockbuster thriller novels that have very short, very engaging chapters, that you find you can't stop reading. Why is that? Well, two reasons: firstly, they have very short chapters so you think to yourself, just one more... and then one more... and next thing you know it is two in the morning. And, secondly, the plot weaves in and out through the structure, rather than being narrated sequentially, so you want to know what happens next – and to find out you have to read on – not just one chapter but maybe a few chapters ahead. Storylines are not resolved until close to the end so there is always a reason to keep reading. You want to find out what happens, so you read on. And on...

You can use these techniques in your book – even if you are writing non-fiction.

Action Step: Weaving In Your Story

Map out your main message or teaching points on one side of the page. And then map out your story or the stories you're telling on the other. These can be case studies, examples, or research studies. You don't have to weave one single story throughout the book. Now link each teaching point with a story – draw a line across or colour code them with highlighter pens. Storytelling doesn't have to be sequential. Tell it by theme, or by how things relate to your teaching points. Just remember that your reader will want to know what happened to your 'character'. If you do weave a single theme or your personal story through the book, remember to close it with a good ending!

Your teaching points	Your personal story
The first teaching point	Who it's about and where it happened
The second teaching point	This happened first
The third teaching point	And you faced these challenges
The fourth teaching point	And then this happened
	Then talk about what challenges you faced at that point, how you over came it, whether there was any additional challenge or setback and how you over came that.
	And then this happened... (you don't need to include all parts of your story!)

Highlight: Highlight the most relevant

Now map your story to your teaching points... use coloured highlighters instead of connecting arrows if you want to

Your teaching points   **Your personal story**

-
-
-
-
-
-

18: **Common Chapter Structure**

When you're writing to teach, it's good to be aware that we all have different learning styles. Different from each other and different from you, the author. For a how-to book, where you are primarily helping your reader achieve or understand something, it can really help to recognise this and to address those different styles in your structure and writing.

I'm going to give you an example of one that I often use and then suggest that you adapt and make it relevant for your book. I usually start with the experience that someone is going to get so that I engage those people who want to know *why* it is important to read or learn. This person usually prefers to experience something before they are prepared to learn more – so I'll explain why they should read and what they will get out of it.

Secondly, I like to write for the ideas person. Someone who loves to engage with concepts – the *what* – level (your typical academic or 'thinker'). This is someone who likes to read to learn, who probably has a lot of books and will talk about them but not necessarily follow-through on the how-to of every single one. This person wants to understand the perspective, and to compare different theories, so facts and figures are helpful, or references to results, or studies. Again, this section doesn't have to be long but there will always be some people who want to see *evidence* before they will believe you.

Thirdly, I'll go into a more detailed *how-to*. This might be the meat of a book – and the reader who loves the how-to will probably have skipped the first two sections because they want to observe and understand the process. They want to do it. Great!

And, finally there are always some learning types who don't need long explanations, they want to dive right in and experiment. *What if...?* This is the person who will assemble the IKEA furniture without reading the instructions... We all know someone like this – you can't change them so make sure you include a short take-away or a *"what if you did this right now?"* teaching point at the end of your chapter.

Holidays with friends!!!

Kate ....

19: **Example Chapter Structure**

Here's how this might flow in an example structure.

Start with Why

Why is it important for your reader to do this step? What reward or benefit will he or she get from reading it? And what might happen if he or she misses out this step or does not follow this advice? What will the experience be?

Let's say you're talking about career development and you have a chapter on *The Importance of Looking Good*. Your 'why' section could cover that a good first impression will get you the job and how a bad dress sense at work means you could be overlooked when managers are thinking about who to promote. How you are going to give them everything they need to dress well and make an impact while feeling good at the same time (no more scratchy suits). This is a great place to introduce your story to get some immediate engagement – how you felt when you walked in a job interview dressed in borrowed clothes for example – connect with the experience they might be having.

Then Some Theory or Facts

Do you have some data or evidence around your topic? Relate a little bit of it here because there are some readers who will need to be convinced that your solution is based in fact before they will believe you or follow your how-to advice. If it's not an academic topic, then talk about your results (or the results of your clients or customers).

Sticking with the career theme, maybe you have some evidence to quote that interviewers typically make a decision in the first thirty seconds of an interview. If you are telling a story then you can talk about your results – the outcomes – what happened. Once you knew the secrets to dressing well to sell yourself, you went for three interviews and were offered all three of the jobs – your CV didn't change but the way you dressed and the way you felt did!

A Solid How-To

And then move on to your teaching part. What is your process? What does your reader need to do first and then next? This will be your longest section. Maybe you start with an assessment of their ambitions and their wardrobe, moving on to a virtual shopping trip. You can talk about the little things that make a difference (accessories?). Or what clothes are appropriate in different work environments – not everyone needs to or wants to dress for corporate. What's your process for knowing how to look your best at all times? How to transition from the interview to the everyday work-wear... and so on.

Mistakes or FAQs

If we focus only on the teaching, we can forget to explain some of the basic things "not" to do. This is a great place to ask questions, or tell stories – tales of what went wrong for you or for your other clients. Opening up to mistakes can be very engaging and humanising for your reader. Knowing what to avoid means he or she is more likely to implement your content and maybe recommend or work with you. What would you want your reader to avoid? Or what questions might they still have?

So in the dress for success theme, it could be, *"worst things to wear in any situation"*, *"what to do if you have an unexpected meeting"*, or *"three things you should always keep in your desk drawer 'just in case'"*. Have some fun – this section doesn't need to be long but relating some mistakes can lighten the tone of a long how-to.

One Action Step or Simple Challenge for Your Reader

I love to leave readers with action steps. Or thought provoking questions. Or reflections. Or repeat your key message. One small piece that they can take away even if they don't read – or remember – the whole chapter. Most people won't take action on your content but if you can leave them with a nugget that is easy to implement and pushes the boundary of what they are comfortable doing then you have done a good job.

A simple one for the career theme could be *whatever you wear, make sure your clothes are clean and fresh every day. Or – Go and get some great quality, well-fitting underwear – if you feel good, you'll look good.*

Feel Free To Adapt!

You don't have to – and probably don't want to – use those titles as your sub-headings. Make them relevant to your content but keep in mind that your readers are going to have different learning styles and setting a clear structure will help you touch all those different styles. One author I've worked with had a medical background before she re-trained as a life coach. She uses the 'Dr' theme in her branding and has kept this going in her book – with self-diagnosis, symptoms, prescription, and re-diagnosis. Be a little bit playful – so long as it's a fit for your brand and business. It's your book – bring your personality into it.

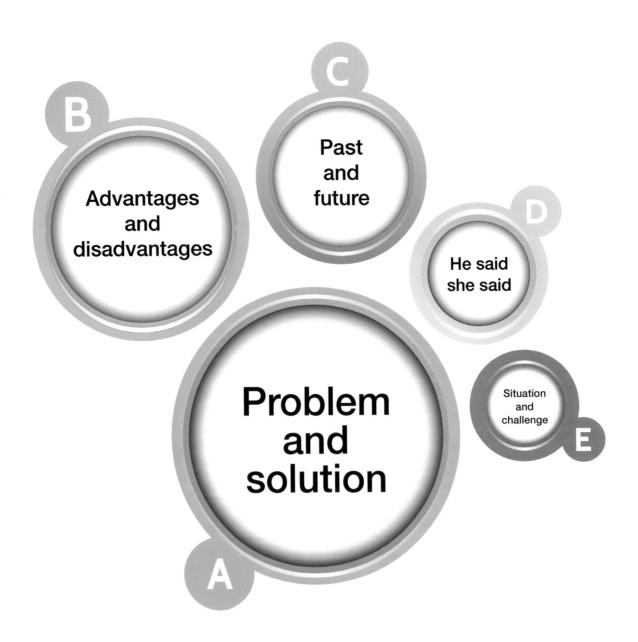

Even If You Don't Have a Process, You Can Still Have Structure

Your book may not follow this detailed structure. You may not have a teaching book, but maybe you want to position yourself as a thought leader or challenge industry thinking? Or you're telling your story. If the structure we just went through doesn't work, that's OK. Just remember that a clear structure helps your reader absorb and use your information. Whatever structure you want to have, plan it out in as much detail as possible at this stage of the process. Here are some other ways you can think about to organise your content into a consistent structure:

A Problem and solution. Outline a problem or a question, and then answer it.

B Advantages and disadvantages. It's easy for a reader to understand the pros and cons of a situation, or a course of action and then you can lead them to a suggested action.

C Past and future. What happened versus what can happen in the future. This is a good way to think about those opinion pieces – your thought leader book.

D He said she said. Not literally but 'compare and contrast' can again be a great way to present facts and help convince readers by telling stories and outcomes or comparing perspectives.

E Situation and challenge. Maybe you want to compare the status quo with what could be? Piece by piece, deconstruct the current thinking in your industry. Then challenge it and compare it to your approach. Explain why that is better and how your reader can move towards it.

Action Step: Revise Your Chapter Structure

Go back to the beginning of this section where you mapped your content into your chapter structure. Revise and refresh it based on these principles. Be ruthless; if it doesn't fit, delete it. Create a common chapter structure. Slot in stories. Work at it until you are ready to write. At this stage, I'd probably be working on a white board or starting to put a structure into a word-processing document.

Let's say you have a seven-step process that you are teaching in your book. Each chapter is one of steps so within each chapter, create a common structure. Do you want to use my suggestion? Or, as you made your mind map or your post-it exercise, were there common words or themes that make sense as a structure? Revise it here.

20: **Communicating Your Message**

This is a section that stands slightly to one side in the process – it's not part of the process of turning what you know into a book, but you might find it useful to return to this section when you start to write. I include it because, while we're not writing yet, I want you to create a good book when you do come to write. And the better you communicate what you know, the more you will transform the lives of those who read it, and the more books you will sell (well, hopefully!) You don't have to be an accomplished writer – what makes good non-fiction is as varied as what makes good fiction but here are a couple of key principles for you to be thinking about and practising.

Connect With Your Reader

The more we understand the person we are writing for, the better a connection we will create. If you communicate from a place of understanding and empathy, you will create common ground with your reader. The more common ground you have the more you can convince them to do what you're asking or the more believable your story will be, and the more easily you will be able to lead them on the next step of the journey or understand the next stage of the process.

With fitness, are they out of breath climbing a flight of stairs, or playing with the children. Or is it hard for them to get a point across in a meeting and they don't feel heard or that their opinion is valued... You'll probably find that they are experiencing something you have already lived through in the context of your book. Does he or she want to be inspired, educated, challenged, nurtured, transformed, understood? Maybe some combination of all of these?

And remember to express your point of view in different ways. One person may connect with facts and logic. Another with emotion and feelings. Have you ever been in class or at work and no matter how many times something is explained, you don't get it? And then someone else chips in and suddenly it's obvious? Choosing different ways to communicate will help more of your readers 'get' your point and understand your ideas.

Get Feedback

We're often terrified of feedback – especially from people we know. But it's much better to give our book to a small group of readers, get some feedback, and then go to print knowing we have put our very best work out there. There will be phrases that people don't understand. There will be sections that really resonate, and sections that are long and hard to follow. Ask for, and use, feedback, and be confident that you will create a better book.

But how to get feedback? Better not to ask family and friends – they'll either be flattering because they support you, or they won't really understand what you're writing about. Instead, when you have a near final draft, bring together a small group of clients or connections – people who are a close fit for your ideal reader. Ask them for honest opinions on your content. Be specific: Were the exercises easy to follow? Were there sections you didn't understand? Most people are generous with their time and will help with this.

Keep It Simple

We've already talked about the concept of *One Book, One Idea*. Keep it simple. If you have a single idea, a simple theme that repeats and develops through your book, then you will write a better book than if you try to scatter a lot of ideas and don't really develop any of them. Your expertise shines through when you show depth. This is not journalism, this is expert positioning.

And think about your language. What's your reader's level of technical knowledge? Is he or she a beginner and is it better to talk about *measuring the economy,* rather than the *UN System of National Accounts*? You want to show that you have authority and leadership, but connect with the vocabulary your reader is using rather than the one that might use when you are giving a talk for your peer group (unless your reader *is* your peer group).

Don't Worry About Your First Draft

The only way to write a good book is to get your ideas onto paper and then improve them. The more you write the better you will get and the more easily you will find *your voice*. And remember – your first draft is not your final draft. People tell me they don't think their writing is any good. Well first of all it's probably better than you think. And second of all, if you hadn't done the first draft, you wouldn't be able to do a second draft. So just see it for what it is – a work in progress. Be pleased that you got your ideas into a structure and then go through, systematically, and edit or re-write, section by section.

And if you'd like some quick exercises to help you get into the flow and practice your writing, then check out my free course Becoming a Writer at **thebigbookproject. com.**

It's OK To Be Challenging

It's OK to be challenging, to be a contrarian. Don't repeat opinions that you know (or believe) not to be true. If you don't agree with something, say it like it is, or like you see it. Expect to be criticised – some people won't like it when you rock the boat, but standing firm can also help you stand out.

Challenge your reader if that's appropriate. If you know that what you are asking them to do is hard, then say so. It can be hard to eat healthy food all the time. Give them the first step, make it manageable, but don't pretend your process is a magic pill if it isn't. Show them why you want them to follow your advice, how to do it, what might go wrong and how to overcome that, and then inspire them to take the first step.

Show Don't Tell

In fiction, writers talk about *'show don't tell'*. You don't say that a character is a bully; you show it by his actions and his dialogue. We can borrow this technique in non-fiction. For example if you're teaching someone some meditation techniques, then use calming language and gentle metaphors to make them feel more relaxed as they follow your process. Talk about what you want them to see and experience in language that evokes those feelings. You don't need to say *"Now relax."* But you can say, *"Close your eyes and take deep breaths while slowly counting to five."* The relaxation will follow from the actions you ask someone to take.

And stories can be really effective here – use case studies to show results, or your story told in stages throughout the book – people remember stories.

Be Open

There is a misconception that we have to be perfect and present a shining example to others. But actually the reverse is true – showing flaws will add dimension and depth to your writing. Your reader is much more interested in your story – and connecting with someone who isn't perfect makes us feel human. Especially if your story resonates with what they are currently experiencing (because we all have flaws!) Ultimately, of course, you want to leave them with hope. But showing a few of your lows as well as your highs shows that success is just as possible for them as it is for you.

21: **Making Time to Write**

The next critical piece is making time to write. The writing part doesn't need to be hard and it doesn't need to take months. I know that most of us are writing around doing something else – a business, or a job, or domestic responsibilities – sometimes all of these – and this is why I put so much emphasis on structure. When you have a structure, you can pick it off section by section and get 'er done.

We often start with high hopes and lofty ambitions. But writing is more about habit and routine than it is about waiting for the inspiration to strike. This section is about helping you create a realistic writing timetable – one that you can stick to it. And I do mean realistic. If it works for you to timetable every 30-minute slot in your diary then go ahead and do that. But if that feels constraining and you know you won't follow it, then set up a regular time to write, that you can stick to *most of the time.* I want you to get this done but I don't want you to be a slave to your computer while you are doing it.

Your final action step in this section is to work out a writing plan. Whatever you decide, I want you to commit – and I want it to be realistic for you. Before we do that, I wanted to share some of my best productivity tips. My best practice writing tips that have taken me years to get right.

Pick a Section

I think we've pretty much covered this, but the idea behind creating a structure is that you will never be lacking in inspiration. If you don't feel inspired, then just pick a section and write. It doesn't have to be linear – I don't write from beginning to end. It doesn't matter which section you pick, it just matters that you start.

Find The Best Place To Write

Where you write can affect your mood. I like to be quiet. You might like music. It's important that you have somewhere to go that gives you a sense of peace and the right environment. That might be at home. It might mean a trip to the local library on a Saturday. But integrate *where* you will write into your plan so you get your best work done with ease.

Write To Time Not To Word Count

We writers talk a lot about word count. About how long our book is and how many words we wrote today. But that can be very intimidating. Instead, I want you to get into the flow of writing. To just write. And to write to a time limit not a word count target. I might set aside an hour, or two hours. And I time myself. I do look at word count at the end. But I am not sitting down with the intention of writing 1,000 or 2,000 words. That part just happens.

You need to know this because we can more easily control the amount of time we spend than the number of words we create. The more you write the more you'll discover what a decent word count is for your writing session. But maybe you are having a bad day and it doesn't flow for some reason. The last thing you need is to feel bad about that. If you work to a time limit, you'll avoid self-criticism because you've done your hour. OK so it didn't feel as good as it did sometimes but you can still be proud that you achieved something and congratulate yourself on the words you did write today.

The Power Hour

I am a morning person. The best time for me to do anything creative (or be my most productive) is when I first sit down. So I often talk about a concept I call the *Power Hour*. This is what it is and I'd encourage you to give it a go. Set aside an hour to get your best work done. Make sure it's an hour *without any distractions* – this is critically important!

Don't check your email; don't have your social media on. Ideally don't even be in range of an internet or phone connection. It might mean that your power hour is first thing in the morning like mine. Or it might be the first hour you are at your writing desk after everyone else has gone to bed. Work out when's best for you and write it down as part of your commitment.

The Two Hour Rule

I know, more rules... But I've designed them to make you ultimately feel freer and enjoy your writing more.

I've found that writing flows best in chunks of two to three hours. I can immerse myself for a full day. But it can be exhausting. I prefer to get something down and then switch tasks so that my brain has time to process what I've written without feeling overwhelmed by new content. I know not everyone can dedicate two or three hour blocks so experiment with the length of time you write for and see what works for you. Break it into hour-long sessions with a ten-minute break in between if you can. But a two to three hour block is ideal if you can dedicate that much time.

Action Step: My Writing Time Is...

Think about the best time for you to write, and then make a written commitment to it. Are you a morning person? Are you a late night writer? Do you prefer to lock yourself away for a single day, maybe at the weekends and have a dedicated stretch of writing time? Be realistic and think about other commitments. On the other hand, if you say you don't have the time it probably means you are prioritising other things. If you don't know where to find the time then keep a time diary for a couple of days and see what comes up. What can you stop doing for a few weeks? Let go of some of the less important things (like TV!) for a couple of months.

Ask for support from those around you. Maybe your partner can do the food shopping for a few weeks. Maybe it's worth getting a cleaner? Maybe you can go to the library and miss junior football all day Saturday for the next six weeks. Small sacrifices will get your book done in less time than you expect.

Write this out in your diary or planner. Block off some time. Think about what you do in the moments before you sit down to write. I want you to create a smooth transition, without any resistance. And think about what small reward you are going to give yourself afterwards. So if you write in the evenings for example, make it easy to go to your room to write by asking your partner if he or she will clear up after you finish your meal every evening for the next two months. And then give yourself a reward of an hour's together time or TV time when you finish. If you integrate your writing habit into your daily routine, you'll find it easier to stick to the writing plan.

Write out your habit in the space below. It can help to get the commitment and support of those around you – they will be more supportive (and there is also a little unspoken accountability!) if they know about your book and they know why it is important to you.

_____

_____

_____

_____

_____

_____

_____

_____

_____

_____

_____

_____

_____

_____

_____

_____

22: **Getting Finished**

It's all very well to have a plan, but sometimes the hardest part is doing it. There are some days when the blank screen or the empty page just seems to grow bigger and more intimidating and the more we stare at it the further away we feel from starting. This is writer's block. We all have those days when we don't feel like writing. Maybe because we have some fear and doubt creep in or maybe we genuinely just don't feel inspired – we're a bit bored to be honest. I know this will happen so I want to shatter any excuses and give you some solutions so you can get over it and get on with it.

What Do You Tell Yourself?

We say a lot of things to ourselves that stop us writing. Stories that we tell ourselves that get in the way of writing – and mostly these are not true or they reflect things that were said in the past and aren't true now.

I believe that most people can write (and that a good editor is an asset to be valued!). A non-fiction book is a collection of what you already do or know. You're not looking for the Nobel Prize for literature. The main thing is to simply decide you're going to write a book, and to have faith that the process isn't as complex or long as you think. I believe in you.

No-One Wants To Read What I Have To Say

Does that question ever come up for you? Either that, or *There are so many books on my topic already – who would want to read mine...?* My advice here is to go and look at your own bookshelf. If there is a subject you're interested in – whether that's cooking, business, or gadgets – how many books do you have? How many recipe books in your kitchen? Business books in your office? Is it more than one? Yes. And very probably it's more than ten. And would you still buy another?

Hold that thought. People want to read *your* idea because it is new. Because it's your personal story. Because of your perspective and expertise. Because they want to learn more, be entertained again, be inspired. Your knowledge is worth more than you think and you deserve to put it into a book.

Notes:

I Don't Have Time to Write

And then there's that old chestnut you don't have the time. Maybe not. But working through this book has shown you how easy it is going to be to put your book together. A few hours planning and your book can probably be written in a few dozen hours total. Whether you spread those over days or weeks is then up to you. If you can commit an hour or two a day for the next few weeks, then you can write a book. Even if you can only commit 15 minutes to write just one small section of your book each day, you will still make progress. Most often, when we say we don't have time, it's either not a priority or we need a little courage or a little bit of structure to create the writing habit. Hopefully you will find solutions to both of these in this book!

Making Time

Often when we procrastinate, we are thinking too much. Writing is a whole brain activity. We use the left side of our brain – which is the part that recognises language – to actually get our words out. And the creative spark comes from the right side of our brain – which is more visually oriented, and where some of the centres of our imagination live. We use both sides of our brain when we write. And if you're constantly analysing yourself, then you're in your left-brain (the thinking part) and not allowing your right brain (the visualisation part) to create. It's like an athlete – when you see an athlete totally in the flow – fully prepared, unconscious about what he or she is doing, just doing it, then those are the moments you'll see a gold medal performance.

This only comes with practice. And habit. Set up regular practices, improve and repeat day after day so that they become second nature to you. The marathon runner does not wait to be inspired to run a marathon. He or she goes out day after day and puts in the training. And writing is much the same. Trust me. It sounds very dull, but ultimately, when it is time to write, we just need to sit down and do it. Have the confidence that inspiration will come when you sit down in front of your desk or computer. Learn not to analyse and your writing will flow quickly and easily. If you find it hard to get started, or if you get to that 80% stage and suddenly feel overwhelmed, then these are my best techniques to get you unstuck and closer to completion.

Go Back To Your Structure

You have a structure in place so that you need never face an empty page. Put your structure into your word processor or a Scrivener file (Scrivener is a writing software that I love to use – highly recommend you check it out). Just pick a section and start. Think of it like writing a blog post or a short note to your reader. Something doable.

A Very Short Time Limit

Sometimes the hours stretching out in front of us seem endless. That's OK. Just write for five minutes and see what happens. Chances are you'll get into the flow. Think of writing like a series of sprints. Don't think about the 30,000 words you 'still' need to write. Think about the next 30 minutes and get your ideas down as fast as you can. If you want a challenge then get an egg timer and write as fast as you can for the three minutes it takes the sand to flow from one side to the other. This exercise is a good way to get over any of that self-talk that might come up. *Who am I to...? Who wants to read my stuff...? Everything has already been written about (insert your topic)...? What if people don't like...?* Just write. These fears are imaginary. You need to take action. Take a deep breath. Know that writing might be new territory for you and that stuff will come up. Just take a few minutes, block out the noise in your head and write.

Go for a Walk

Most of the time it's better to start than to put something off. But occasionally there is a real reason we can't seem to get a particular section down on paper. Go for a walk or a swim or do some other activity that will take your mind completely off writing. I find that something that involves movement or exercise is better than sitting still. Clear your head and something may come up. Or it may not and you just need to go back to the egg timer.

Make It Fun

Some of us are highly motivated by our enjoyment of the actual work we are doing. If you find writing boring, then find a way to make it fun. Brainstorm your ideas with a friend or colleague. Get your assistant to write these up and create your first draft. Play around with pictures and post-its and plan it out so that the writing is just about capturing those ideas on paper. Go and do your work in a coffee shop – your environment is also important to the quality of your work and how much you are motivated to write every day!

Notes:

Get Help

Sometimes we get bogged down with questions. *What's the publishing process? What choices do I have? How on earth do I launch and market my book?*

This is all just stuff that you don't know (yet). Start to ask questions. Read books and find someone who knows more than you know and can give you the right advice. People have written and published books before, and there are experts who can give you connections and information that will answer all of your questions. Don't let the not knowing hold you back. When you feel uncertain or overwhelmed, or you don't understand the process and what you should do next, then reach out to someone who can guide and support you.

And if it's about accountability – goodness knows we all work better to deadlines and commitment to others – then set up some support for your writing. Hire a coach or a mentor, or have an informal arrangement with a friend or a colleague who also has a task they want to complete and check in with each other once a week to stay on track.

Get Back In Touch With Why

Sometimes we need to see how the things we are doing every day are contributing to the bigger picture. If you can see how all of the small steps you take and how every 1,000 words you write contribute to your dream, then you will be more motivated. Get back in touch with why you are writing and why you want to get your message out. Go back to that book cover with your name on it. Put a picture of it, or of what finishing it means to you, somewhere that you will see every day. Your desk, or the fridge, or the bathroom mirror! The more you can feel it and the more vivid the picture, the more motivated you will be to achieve it. Set a date for your book launch party. Think about who will be there. What will they be wearing? What food will you have? Where is it? Create some visuals if you want – draw up a little book launch plan. Make it real. You deserve the success and others deserve to be reading your material. What you have is valuable – get it out into the world.

Journal Some Questions

It can be immensely powerful sometimes to go back to writing longhand. Maybe at the beginning of the writing process, just to get you started. And if you hit 'the wall' or you're stuck, then take a notepad, go somewhere quiet – out into the garden or the park, or a very quiet cafe. And just write. If you don't know where to start then start with a question. *Why am I stuck? Which part of the book should I do next? How can I help myself get beyond this phase? What's important to me about finishing?*

A Damn Good Edit

Sometimes – especially near the end, you need to stop adding new material and thrash through what you already have. You can do this yourself, or you can get an editor to help you. If you're going to do it all yourself, then print out your material. Spread it around the floor or find a large space on a table. Write each chapter title on one single piece of paper and lay these out in order.

Now take some coloured pens or post-it notes and go back to your draft. Colour code or physically move around which section goes into which chapter. Use coloured highlighters to identify what content goes into which sections. Or use a pair of scissors and literally cut up your paper into sections and move them around and staple them together again so you can do that final edit. When you've got all the material for each chapter in place, then take that pile and organise it chapter by chapter. But what if there's material left over that doesn't seem to fit anywhere? Don't worry – you have the beginnings of your next book! Cut it from this version of your book and save it in another document or folder.

It can also help at this stage to write a strong introduction. Focus on eliminating anything that doesn't fit with your introduction. Again – save it for the next book!

Action Step: Which Are Your Top Procrastination Busters?

*Although you are still at the planning stage, there might come a time when you hit a bump. Keep track of a couple of solutions that will get you through when you need them. Which are your top three choices to get unstuck? You will have things you prefer and things that don't seem to be a fit. Make some notes here. Figure out who you can call. Enrol in the writing exercises' class at **thebigbookproject.com**. Buy a timer. Because preparation is key to success.*

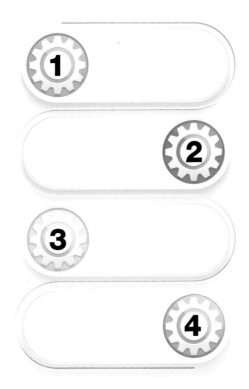

Highlight: Highlight the one or two you will try first

At the end of this chapter:

- You know exactly what single promise you will deliver on in your book. One book – one clear message.

- You have the right flow to your book – your high-level chapter outline.

- You'll have 'shape' to your book – a detailed structure and a full outline of your content. It isn't quite writing by numbers but once you have this the writing will be easy.

- You understand how to connect with your reader, how to make your content engaging so that they want to read on and stay with you.

- You know exactly how to stay focused, banish writer's block and finish the book!

The Book Launch

23: **Introducing You**

I know we see books as intensely personal – and that's where we started, with your why and with your story. But it's also important to sell books – to think strategically about how your book is going to generate more business, raise your profile and achieve the impact you want. And to do this your book has to be noticed. And being noticed is your job. Even if you have a publisher, this role will still fall largely to you.

This short section will help you prepare for that by working out – in advance – a few messages you can share and actions you can take now that will make a big difference when you launch. We'll look at how to build your base of fans and followers. We'll think about creative ways to release content that builds a buzz and generates fascination. And we'll look at the most important places to be when you launch.

Introducing The Author

As you get further ahead with the writing process, I want you to think of yourself as an author. You're not just the business person, the consultant, nutritionist, or personal trainer. You're an author. And you need to say so. You already know you're going to publish, and you know what your book's about. So simply add a line or two to your website and especially to your email signature, to introduce yourself as an author.

Action Step: Create Your New Email Signature

Notes:

The easiest thing you can do right now, is to create a new email signature. This is the text you put at the end of your emails. Just fill in the blank below and start to use it!

Your Name

_____

_____

_____

Forthcoming author of

(insert your book title)

_____

_____

_____

_____

_____

_____

How easy was that? Add this to your website as well. Maybe you can create a page or a post on why you are writing? The final shape of your book isn't finished, but you definitely know the why and it can create strong connections to talk about this, especially if your book has a personal story to it. Plus, people will begin to think of you as a published author even before your book is out.

The Engagement Pitch

I also want you to be introducing yourself in a way that leads naturally to a conversation about your book. It can take a leap of confidence to talk about something that is not yet complete, but it will make it feel real. When people ask the inevitable *'What do you do?'* have a few short words that invite questions. *I'm writing my first book...* will probably lead to an *Oh that sounds interesting, what's it about?* And then you are in conversation mode, not presentation mode. As an author – or soon to be author! – get into the habit of talking about your book. This is about practice for you as much as it is about promotion. As you prepare to launch, you will naturally spark the interest of and create engagement with people you meet. And you'll meet people who will be excited to share – building a network of connections who will support you when you launch.

So rather than I AM a homoeopathist, try...
I'm *writing* my first book
I'm *writing* a book to help women in menopause find natural solutions that work no matter what else you have tried. I want to save women the heartbreak that I've been through trying to find a solution. (A subtle 'why' makes this more powerful but be careful – too much sharing can be off-putting!)

An engaging introduction will invite questions and give you an opportunity to mention your book. Don't force it, but maybe it will create an opportunity for you to offer an advance copy? And when you send out these advance copies, how about a personal or handwritten note to (very subtly) remind the recipient about the connection between the two of you? That way they are more likely to read and (hopefully!) respond back to you.

Action Step: Your Engaging Author Introduction

Brainstorm some phrases that invite questions. Think about using active verbs. I am training for..., I am learning..., I am looking for...

Highlight: Highlight your favourite

24: **Introducing Your Book**

Test Your Book Title

Even though you've already thought of your title, and it may change as you write, it can be a good idea to reflect whether your title is going to help or hinder book sales (and yes, a bad title will sell less well). You don't have to follow an exact formula with your title but just reflect whether it follows these principles.

Is It Clear?

Is it obvious what your book is about? Catchy titles can be fun but – especially if you plan to sell online – a title that says what the book is about is more likely to get you sales. Use the sub-title to clarify what the book's about, your solution and who might be interested. A few that I picked randomly off the bestseller lists include: *Wheat Belly: Lose the Wheat, Lose the Weight, and Find Your Path Back to Health; Boundaries: When to Say YES, When to Say NO, To Take Control of Your Life; Decisive: How to Make Better Choices in Life and Work.* Are you noticing a pattern? A title – short and catchy, not too cute – then a longer subtitle – explaining exactly what the book is about and often with action words (Lose The...).

Does It Invite Desire?

Is there a hint of that emotionally driven desire? *Desirable: Don't Let Love Pass You By* plays on a fear – real or imagined – that love may indeed be passing us by. Don't be threatening, but appeal to the emotionally driven desire and possible unspoken fear that your reader may have. *Kiss Your BUT Good-Bye: How to Get Beyond the One Word That Stands Between You and Success.* Who doesn't want success? And this title shows us that it's easy to achieve by ditching one word from our vocabulary... yet there is an unwritten implication that we may not yet have the success we want.

Interest or Curiosity

Does your title spark interest? You can be clear and still add a twist that will make your reader want to look inside and find out more. How can you incite a little curiosity? *To Sell Is Human: The Surprising Truth About Moving Others. Surprising Truth...* implies that we are going to be told something we don't know or don't expect. It definitely makes me want to know more!

Action Step: Test Your Title

Titles are a great thing to test on your friends and colleagues and clients. Use what they say as feedback. Don't tell them what the book's about yet – if you have to explain it, then you should probably change it. It's really interesting to see what people come up with on their own. In reality a potential customer would see your book in context – on a shelf, or on a website alongside other books, plus they'd have the cover to guide them – so take this exercise as it's meant to be – light-hearted and informative rather than rigorously scientific!

You have lots of time and space to play with your title before you put your book to bed. Some authors even advertise competing title choices (Tim Ferris was notable for this) to see which one is likely to be the more popular choice. You don't need to go that far, but it's a good idea to test your title because what sounds cool and catchy to us can be confusing and off-putting to a potential reader.

What was the feedback?

The Blurb (Or Description)

Your book blurb is simply what goes on the back cover of your print book and what goes into your online description if you're listing online. Write this before you finish the book because the more you write, the more ideas you'll get and a good description will keep you focused. You want to deliver your Big Promise, nothing more, nothing less. Remember, one book, one clear message.

Action Step: Describe Your Book

Here's a format for your blurb, just fill in the gaps...

1. *Attention-grabbing headline – **a promise, a quote, or a claim***

2. *Endorsements – **craft imaginary endorsements from someone you admire (this will inspire you to write the best book possible!)***

3. *Results – what are you going to deliver for your reader? Use bullet-points perhaps?*

-
-
-
-
-
-
-
-
-
-

4. *Call to action – ask them to go ahead and buy! You can be subtle about this and you can frame it as if they have already taken the action you want – 'when you've read this book, you'll be able to imagine / implement / understand...'*

25: **Build The Buzz**

In the internet world, you don't need to wait for the traditional media to pick up your story. You have created and published your book and now you can create your own publicity. You want to let people know that something is coming; create a little excitement, desire and some 'reasons why' someone should engage with you, and buy your book when it comes out. And although you are *writing* for one reader, you are going to be *marketing* to more than one reader.

Think about books you love – there will be expressions or phrases that you touch you, or make you laugh, and that you'd love to discuss with the author. It will be the same for your readers and you can build a community of people who love your messages, want to connect with you, and will be ambassadors for your book.

Anticipation cannot be forced but it can be planned. Relationships cannot be imposed but they can be nurtured. Can you give more to your inner circle than you share with others? And maybe this will come back to you in the future. A blog feature, an introduction, or an invitation to speak. This is also the time to be testing different posts, different messages and different ways of engaging to see what resonates.

I know your focus is on the book, and I know there are only so many hours in a day. It's OK to put this off but if you are able to give a bit of thought to these action steps then you'll come up with better marketing ideas and more time to implement them.

Be Consistent
It's usually just at the point where you think you're repeating yourself, that your ideas take off. The reality is that most people haven't heard your message, or didn't take action on it. Stay 'on message' consistently until you hear people repeating your ideas back to you – that's when you know you're being heard.

As you build anticipation, do it around a small number of key messages that can be repeated and remembered. In other words, create your own sound-bites. Think about successful political campaigns – the focus is on a small number of key commitments, not the full spectrum of what the politician or party stands for. Choice can be overwhelming, so – like politicians – keep your campaign simple and stay consistent.

In *Outliers*, Malcolm Gladwell talks about the 10,000 hour rule – that it takes 10,000 hours to master a skill to the level of genius. He didn't invent this, he's simply reporting it. Yet he does it with such clarity and skill that it's the most-quoted idea from the book and he is the person who is associated with it, rather than the original researchers.

Simple Can Work Best

Complexity can work against you. Books that take off are not always the cleverest or the best written; they are well communicated and well marketed. Strip your idea down to its simplest form. Use one single message – or a set of core messages, and communicate them clearly. People remember what is simple and relevant. Think about books that become phenomena – they often have a small number of simple concepts or instructions that can be easily re-told.

It's Never Too Soon To Start

Get the timing right. Start too early and you risk people losing interest; too late and you can miss opportunities. But don't over-think it. Whatever your reach – whether it's a facebook page of a few thousand or a customer list of a few hundred, start there. Develop your core messages and then release them to the audience you have as you get closer to your launch.

Communication Is More Powerful When It's Two Way

We're no longer in a world of one-way communication. So much of our marketing is about dialogue and engagement. It's no longer enough to have one-way sales messaging. You need to listen and respond as well as talk.

And go further. Use the power of community to help people who are interested in your content and personality come together with you and with each other. This might be your own website, a blog, a forum you manage, a Google Community, or a physical office or community space. And if all this sounds very grand then start small. Host a coffee morning, set up a facebook group. And encourage the people who join you to become leaders themselves. You don't need to be there all of the time – empower others in the process and your community will grow organically.

Notes:

Action Step: Create Your Marketing Messages

We need a few simple messages – newsworthy and nicely packaged. Something short, catchy and memorable. And while you can't guarantee that people will talk about you, you can set up your content so that it makes it easier for people to share.

1. *What is your one big message or Big Promise? Write it in the centre of the diagram.*

2. *What other ideas to you talk about in the book? Write these in the smaller circles.*
What snippets of information might spark someone's interest? Can you distil five core messages or storylines out of your content? Remember – consistency and simplicity are key. Ask yourself, are they interesting and potentially newsworthy? Are they relevant for your audience? Do they invoke curiosity? Are they memorable? What's in your personal story? What's a shared history or a shared passion your reader might have? What music have you been listening to as you write? Or is your book set in a time where you can bring in references to popular culture?

3. *Who might connect with these ideas or stories? Write some ideas in the blank space around the outside of the diagram opposite.*
Who is in a similar place to you when you started? Can you empathise with the mother, or full-time employee who is trying to escape the corporate world? Someone with the same taste in music or fashion as yourself? If you're writing a book about maintaining optimum nutrition and you yourself are a parent, you can probably empathise with the busy working mum who does not have a lot of time to spend on complicated recipes.

That doesn't mean that only busy working mothers are going to buy your book. That's just one connection with one person. You're also writing for the juice fan who wants to know about the latest trends in juicing. And the gadget junkie who wants to know what kit you use. And the person who wants to be unconventional and hear what's special or remarkable or new about your approach.

How can you create messages that work for all of these people individually? And bring those messages into play over time to build anticipation?

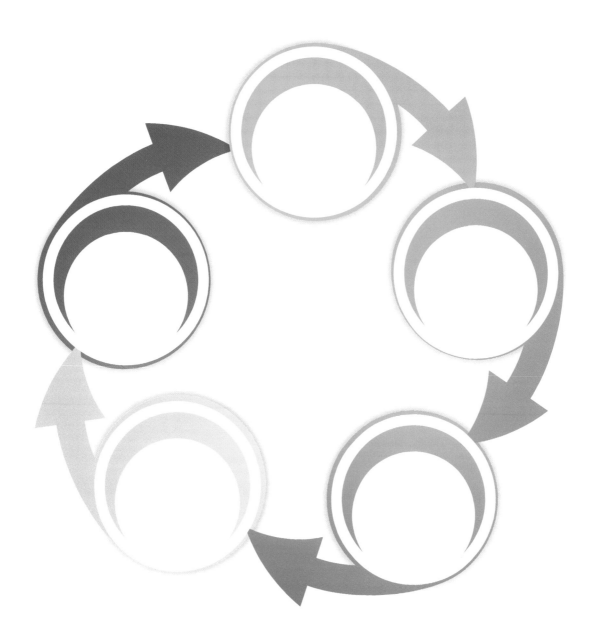

Action Step: Where Are Your Fans?

Where can you find these people and how do you communicate with them?
Write your ideas on the opposite page.

Especially online, we have such a great choice of media to communicate what we have to say. Do you like to write? Will people come to your blog, or see your facebook posts? Do you like to make or to watch video? Then YouTube might be the perfect place for you. You may want to post links to videos of people who have inspired you to write, or your own content. Have you been listening to music as you write? How about setting up playlists of music you've been listening to and how it's really bringing back memories of a certain event you're writing about? Post these on your social media or create a playlist on iTunes.

Think about focus at first. Identify a few key channels for your communication and then prepare some consistent and engaging content. It's better to have 2,000 blog readers and no facebook page, than to spread yourself too thinly and make little or no impact on any of your platforms. It's easier to move people to other channels when you have a critical mass on one channel.

And then just post your content... Start to see what gets noticed and do more of what works. It's a great testing ground for launch day.

THE BOOK LAUNCH

26: **It's Launch Time!**

When it comes to launching, the more people are talking about you, the more notice you'll get. If you've been building anticipation, then now is the time to consolidate it. You've created a community; left tasters and teasers to interest and engage them. And now it's about reach – how far you can spread your message.

The power of our networks isn't just about our direct connections; it's the connections of our connections. It's more powerful – for example – for me to reach out to the leader of a business organisation whose members might want to write a book, than it is to try to connect with those members one by one.

You can do the same. It's easier to sell 'we' and the more people you have to help with this, the more you will multiply your impact. By engaging a bigger community, you have the potential to reach thousands or tens of thousands. Nurture your connections, put out interesting and important content. Things that are relevant, special, or challenging, and certainly thoughtful and intelligent. And value each contact you have. It's the personal touch that people will remember and respect you for – and ultimately the more likeable and trustworthy you are the more saleable your book becomes.

Action Step: Engage Your Community – Who Do You Know?

1. *Who do you know and where do you meet people who will be interested in talking about your book? Are they small business owners at the chamber of commerce meeting? Subscribers to your blog? People in your facebook groups? Mums at the school gate? Your work colleagues? Write these along the arrows in the diagram opposite.*

2. *Ask yourself, who are the connections of your connections? Think of how you can connect with their networks and connections, rather than connecting directly with potential customers. Map this out in the spaces between the arrows.*

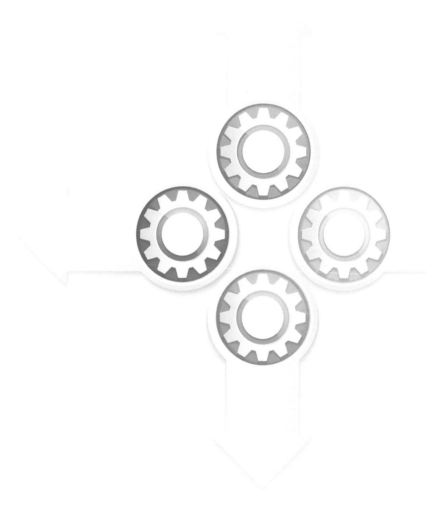

Notes:

Your launch is simply a coordinated set of messages over a few days or even hours and the aim of any launch is to get as many people as possible talking about and buying your book in as short time-span as possible. You've got everything you need to do that.

You've been building your base, connecting and engaging with your audience, and you have a great book. Now you're ready to announce it to the world! However, if you're just starting to think about this for the first time as you launch your book then don't worry. Start where you are. You have plenty of time and the race does not finish after the launch party.

Your launch might be an in-person event (a great way to celebrate your book and the completion of that part of the process) or you might want to party online with a virtual event, or run a series of promotions back to your book. You want to get noticed – whether it's in the Amazon.com rankings or in the media or amongst your network of contacts. You already have your core messages, you've tested posts and communication to see what gets the most engagement so this is your final activity. Do this closer to the actual launch – I usually start to think about this in detail when I send my book off to the editor and I have a period of time when it's literally taken out of my hands.

Action Step: The Launch Plan

OK let's take this final step:

Identify three core messages or 'sound-bites' – which ones have been working best and which messages seem to get the most notice.

Think of them like headlines. If you follow my diet plan you'll lose ten pounds in five weeks and never have cravings again. Or, "It is possible to run a marathon after fifty, even if you've never run a mile before." Or, "It's possible to get that promotion that's been eluding you, just by changing the way you dress."

Notes:

And then think of at least ten places you want to be seen and be talked about. Meetings. Blogs. Media. Radio. Other people's social media stream. If you could choose ten dream places to have your book previewed or reviewed or talked about, online and offline, what are they? There's no reason to stop at ten, this can be just a start. The more connections you have the more choosy you can be about where to appear. Pick the ones which will get you the biggest impact. But for a first book we're often happy to appear anywhere that someone will have us! Remember to coordinate efforts around your launch. For at least a day try to "be everywhere" because this will get you the most buzz online and offline.

And then it's simply a case of setting a date, getting into action and being willing to go for it. And remember to celebrate. This is an amazing achievement, one that so many people want and so few finish – you are now a published author – something to be very proud of!

27: **The End...**

So this is the end of one part of the journey and the beginning of the next...

You have all your ideas captured, filtered, checked against your priorities, and recorded in one place.

You are ready to write.

Go back to the section on writing and set up your writing habits. Make a commitment to yourself and to someone else (so that it is very real) and then simply start. There is no reason at all to wait. The timing will never be more perfect than it is right now – you are ready. We've taken a shapeless, unformed mush of an idea (and yes this is a technical writing term!) and created a clear flow to your book, a detailed structure and writing plan, and the beginnings of your launch plan. I want you to be proud of the work you've put in and I want you to see how achievable and – hopefully – easy, it's going to be to put your book together.

28: **What's Next?**

If you'd like to stay connected with me then you can go to my website at **thebigbookproject.com**. If you need any extra support or accountability, you can connect with me and I'll be happy to let you know whether I can help you. If you'd like to check out my courses and workshops, I'd love to see you there. Above all, enjoy the process and do please let me know when you're launching your published book!

At the end of this chapter:

- You know how to introduce yourself as an author and talk about your book so that you hold attention and make someone want to learn more.

- You have the formula for a bestselling book title – model success and you will make it easy for your readers to know what your book is about before they buy it.

- You know how to build buzz around your book and create a community of people who will support you when you launch.

- You have your core marketing messages mapped out and – importantly – you know how to get them into the world so that the right people see and hear them.

- And finally you've set a date for your book launch. Congratulations!

Personal Notes:

Personal Notes:

About the Author:

Cathy Presland is an author, speaker and mentor to entrepreneurs who want to write a book as part of their business (or personal) growth strategy. Whether you want to write as an expert to position your business, or to share your message – and best of all when there's a link between the two. "Marketing is a credibility game" as one of her students said and there is nothing that will boost your credibility faster than having a good book.

For over twenty years Cathy has been an economic adviser to governments around the world. Her career has spanned setting up a micro-lending fund for women in Africa, to managing multi-billion programmes of economic development funding for European governments. Today her ambitions are to help you create a business and life you love so that you can be inspired to do the big stuff.

You can find out more about Cathy at thebigbookproject.com